Meet Rev. George

MW00989708

both the pulpit and the printed page. Since 1992 Rev. Malkmus has brought his ministry to the world via seminars, newsletters, books, and radio and television appearances— including two appearances on the 700 Club and the Trinity Broadcasting Network or "TBN."

Rev. Malkmus became a Christian at a Billy Graham Crusade Rally in New York City in 1957. After spending four years in preparation for the ministry, he spent 20 years pastoring churches in New York, North Carolina, Florida, and Tennessee, and founded both a Christian school and Bible Institute. His radio broadcast, "America Needs Christ," aired for more than 15 years.

Then, in 1976, at the height of his ministry, colon cancer struck. Having just watched his mother die of the same disease following brutal chemotherapy and radiation treatments, Rev. Malkmus rejected the world's approach to the curing of disease and instead turned to the Genesis 1:29 diet of uncooked fruits and vegetables and carrot juice.

Following God's way instead of man's way, Rev. Malkmus healed himself in one year of not only his cancer, but also all other physical problems. He has remained free of any sickness of any kind for over 20 years. Because of what he experienced and learned, he has felt an ever greater and burning desire to share with the world the message "You don't have to be sick."

Realizing the traditional medical approach was not the answer to man's ills, Rev. Malkmus has spent the last 20 plus years learning everything he could about alternative health. He has done extensive Biblical research; studied with Dr. Carey Reams in Georgia; worked with Dr. Ann Wigmore in Boston; spent two years learning Natural Hygiene and lecturing at the Shangri-La Health Resort in Florida. He has studied most modalities in both the traditional and alternative health fields.

The author of two best-selling books, *Why Christians Get Sick* and *God's Way to Ultimate Health*, Rev. Malkmus currently publishes a health magazine with a circulation of 200,000. He appears regularly on television and radio shows and conducts health seminars throughout the world. Rev. Malkmus is founder and President of Hallelujah Acres, a worldwide ministry teaching health from a Biblical perspective.

On May 5, 1995, Rev. Malkmus received an honorary Doctorate Degree in Literature from Louisiana Baptist Seminary for his work in Biblical Nutrition.

You Don't Have to be Sick!
a Christian Health Primer

by Rev. George H. Malkmus

The nutritional and health information in this book is based on the teachings of God's Holy Word, the Bible, as well as research and personal experience by the author and others. The purpose of this book is to provide information and education about health. The author and publisher do not directly or indirectly dispense medical advice or prescribe the use of fasting or diet as a form of treatment for sickness without medical approval. Nutritionists and other experts in the field of health and nutrition hold widely varying views. The author and publisher do not intend to diagnose or prescribe. The author and publisher intend to offer health information to help you cooperate with your doctor or other health practitioners in your mutual quest for health. In the event you use this information without your doctor's or health practitioner's approval, you prescribe for yourself. This remains your constitutional right. The author and publisher assume no responsibility.

© Copyright 1999 by George H. Malkmus
Cover Design and Layout by Shannon Brown

All rights reserved

Visit our web site at http://www.hacres.com

Tenth printing 2004
ISBN 0-929619-05-6

This Edition Published and Distributed by

Hallelujah Acres Publishing
P.O. Box 2388
Shelby, NC 28151
704-481-1700

Dear Christian Friend:

Let's get right down to brass tacks regarding health and health care:

The World's Way Is Killing Us.

You know what I mean because if you're like just about every other Christian, you or a family member or a friend has a serious physical problem which requires the care of a medical doctor.

I hate to say it, but chances are good that the person under this doctor's care is not getting better. In fact, too many of our loved ones are getting worse because of the drug, cut, and burn approach of modern medicine.

But what about the statements we hear on the television news almost every night that the current health care system is the best ever?

Wrong.

We don't have a health care system—we have a disease care system, and it's not very effective.

- Heart disease still ranks as the No. 1 killer
- Cancer kills men, women, and children at ever increasing rates
- More people are developing diabetes than ever before
- Arthritis is crippling hundreds of thousands every year
- Autoimmune diseases are running rampant

And what is the medical profession doing about all this?

As usual, it's keeping its public relations machine well-oiled while singing the same old tune about new cures that are just around the corner.

Most of us have grown up hearing promises about cures for this and miracle drugs for that.

But where are these cures?

Are the miracle drugs we hear so much about actually curing people? Or are these drugs being quietly removed from the pharmacies some years later because of the harmful effects they are having on people?

If the medical doctors really had the answers, why are we getting sicker and sicker while the cost of health care tops a trillion dollars each year?

If the world's medical system really worked, why do ever increasing numbers of our children have to take Ritalin to make it through a school day? And why is it that children on Ritalin often develop new and even worse problems?

If the current medical system really worked, why can't the doctors heal the many people diagnosed with diseases like Fibromyalgia and Chronic Fatigue Syndrome and Candidiasis?

If the world's medical system really worked, why are ever increasing numbers of women being diagnosed with breast cancer while prostate cancer is epidemic among men?

If the world's system really worked, why are so many drugs (with their often horrible side effects) causing so many problems? In an April 1998 article in the *Journal of the American Medical Association*, we learn that over 100,000 Americans die each year just from the side effects of these doctor-prescribed drugs while over two million have to be hospitalized.

If the world's system really worked, why, according to the October 28, 1998, issue of the *Journal of the American Medical Association*, are an estimated 180,000 people killed each year by medical mistakes that largely go unreported?

Incredibly, according to their own flagship journal, the medical community acknowledges almost 300,000 drug and doctor-caused deaths each year. This figure makes the current worldly medical system the third highest <u>cause</u> of death in America.

In short, if we have the best health care system in history, why do people continue to be so sick, and why are over 90% of the prayer requests in our churches for sickness?

Because the World's Way doesn't work.

The World's Way continues to walk us down a path that leads away from God and the beautiful garden He originally placed us in, instead of back to it.

There is another way, a better way of taking care of our physical bodies, and that is God's way. I used this method on myself over 20 years ago to heal my colon cancer, and I've spent the past two decades sickness-free while refining the details.

If you're ill and your doctor no longer knows what to do to try to help you, you don't have to travel to some "world-renown clinic" where they'll charge you thousands of dollars for complicated tests to diagnose some disease that they then probably can't do anything about other than to cut you open, burn you with radiation, or inject into your bloodstream derivatives of toxic chemicals used in World War I to kill soldiers.

My friend, all too often the accepted procedures of the World's System for serious disease do more harm than good.

You see, man has complicated everything about disease. From his Latin prescriptions and his million dollar cat-scan machines to his scientific studies and double-blind research, modern medicine's quest for the truth has only led us deeper into the jungle of ignorance.

What does the Bible have to say about this world's system?

"For the wisdom of this world is foolishness with God." (1 Corinthians 3:19)

"And be not conformed to this world: but be ye transformed by the renewing of your mind, that ye may prove what is that good, and acceptable, and perfect, will of God." (Romans 12:2)

"And a certain woman, which had an issue of blood twelve years, And had suffered many things of many physicians, and had spent all that she had, and was nothing bettered, but rather grew worse." (Mark 5:25-26)

But there is a way out.

At Hallelujah Acres we've discovered a natural approach that conforms to God's laws. An approach that leads us back to the garden of health and happiness instead of further into the forest of disease and despair.

To be honest, the solution to illness is simple, so simple you may find it shocking.

I can state the solution in one sentence:

If you stop putting into your body the things that created the problems and instead give your body the nutrients it needs to rebuild, your diseases will almost always go away (if the medical approach hasn't already destroyed your immune system with drugs, chemotherapy, radiation, and/or surgery).

Our experience at Hallelujah Acres with tens of thousands of people has been that, in most instances, disease is caused by wrong food and lifestyle choices—the poor choices we each make when we live man's way instead of God's way.

Unfortunately, although abundant research and scientific evidence confirming the diet/disease connection already exists, traditional medicine pretty much ignores it.

Hallelujah Acres offers an alternative.

Unlike other non-traditional approaches to health which urge you to take minerals for this, herbs for that, and vitamins for something else, in these pages you'll learn exactly what you can do to restore your health God's way instead of man's way.

We at Hallelujah Acres have discovered a better way. A simple way based on God's natural laws. A way that deals with the cause of physical problems rather than the symptoms.

And guess what happens when people try our way?

They almost always get well, and we have tens of thousands of testimonies to support this statement.

People are getting well by droves, and some of them get well so fast we can hardly believe it. Others take longer. But we estimate that over 90% of the individuals who try the Hallelujah Diet and lifestyle for at least six months either improve significantly or heal completely.

People who have spent thousands and thousands of dollars only to be told by the medical system to "get your affairs in order" have tried our program as a last resort. Today, many of them are still alive, experiencing superior health and sharing their healing experience with others.

You're going to hear from several of these individuals later in this book. That's right. The medical profession had even given some of them up for dead.

Well, God's way doesn't give anyone up for dead. At Hallelujah Acres, we teach there's always hope and that once you stop putting into your body those things that created the physical problem and instead provide your body with the proper building materials and living conditions, the chances are very good you will get well.

Here's a true statement regarding God's plan for His people:

You Don't Have to Be Sick!

But before I get into the details of what you may choose to do to ward off disease for the rest of your life, I'd like to explain why I'm devoting my life and ministry to sharing this health message.

Here's what sparked my interest in Biblical health.

In 1957, at the age of 23, I became a Christian and shortly thereafter was called by God into the Gospel Ministry, and off I went for four years of preparation. During those years of schooling, I thought I was being taught everything I would ever need to know to successfully pastor and lead God's people. I remember the day I graduated and the confidence I had, thinking I had been taught everything I would ever need to know to be a successful pastor. Boy, was I ever in for a rude awakening!

Shortly after accepting God's call to my first church, I was faced with something for which my schooling had not prepared me—how to deal with physical problems. As people in my congregations became sick, I repeatedly asked myself: "What do I do? How do I deal with these physical problems for which I've had no preparation?"

Well, I did what I had seen other Christians and pastors do over the years in various churches I had attended. I prayed for their healing and asked others to pray also. But often, after abundant and fervent prayer, I saw Christians continuing to get sicker. I asked myself, "What do I do now?"

You see, my mother was a registered nurse, and Mom had always taught me that when you get sick, you go to the doctor and do what he says. So after prayer had failed, I would encourage people to go to the doctor. I would find myself, as their pastor, visiting them in their home or in the hospital and asking God to give the doctor wisdom to know what drug to prescribe. But all too often, the doctor was not able to help them either, and I saw many Christians die—some as children, others in the very prime of life. Now what does a pastor do?

For this next step, I had been prepared in my schooling: I had been taught how to conduct a funeral. And so, if the person who had died was a Christian, I would seek to comfort and encourage at the funeral by telling the bereaved that their loved one was in a better place. For the elderly believer, this ceremony was not difficult for their funeral was like a graduation celebration.

But one of the hardest things I ever did was to conduct the funeral for a 24-year old mother of two who died following a bout with breast cancer, leaving behind a husband and two young children. How does a pastor handle this type of funeral or that of a baby or teenager when they die of some disease? Does it comfort the bereaved to tell them that this was just 'God's will'? Or do we say that we don't understand and only when we get to heaven will all these things be revealed. Is it not strange that my schooling had prepared me for ministering to the living after a loved one had died, but not how to minister to that deceased person before they died?

Sickness among Christians continued to be a thorn in my flesh during most of my 20 years of ministry as I pastored in five different churches to many thousands of people. I did not understand why Christians were just as sick as non-Christians. But I was soon to find the answer to that question the hard way.

My personal testimony of healing

In 1976, at the age of 42, I was pastoring a very successful church in upstate New York. I had started the church in 1970 with an advertisement in the local paper that we were starting a Bible-believing church. On the first Sunday we had 50 people in attendance. The church grew rapidly and by 1976 had reached a membership of more than 600 with assets of over a quarter million dollars. We also had a Christian School, grades K-12, along with a Bible Institute program. Our radio broadcast, *America Needs Christ*, was heard on many radio stations each week, and we had over a dozen young people in school preparing for the ministry. God's blessing was so abundantly evident on this ministry. Well, at this high point in my ministry I was told I had colon cancer.

I was shocked. I didn't understand. How could God bless the ministry so abundantly and allow something like this to happen? I searched my life to see if there was something I had done or failed to do for which God was punishing me. But to the best of my knowledge I was serving the Lord with a pure heart and a clean life. I asked, "Why Lord are you allowing me to have this potentially life threatening physical problem?" Obviously, I did not understand physical sickness in my own life any better than I had understood it in the lives of the people to whom I ministered. I didn't know what to do.

Just prior to my being told I had colon cancer, I had watched my own mother die following a bout with colon cancer. Mother, being a registered nurse, had great faith in her doctors when they told her that her only hope of surviving her cancer was to yield to their treatments of chemotherapy, radiation, and surgery. And thus she willingly accepted her doctor's treatments. When mother was first diagnosed, there was no outward sign that she had a physical problem. But it wasn't long after she started those treatments that she rapidly deteriorated physically and ultimately died.

At the time of Mother's passing, I was convinced it was not the cancer that caused her death, but the treatments she had received at the hands of the medical profession. So now I really faced a dilemma. Mother had always taught me to trust and follow doctor's orders. And yet I had witnessed the horrible results that followed her medical treatment. Should I subject my body to the same medical procedures I felt had caused Mother's death?

It was at this point that I turned my back on the medical approach to physical problems and went searching for an alternative. In my search, I remembered an evangelist in Texas by the name of Lestor Roloff. He was a great Gospel preacher but was also considered by many to be a Health Nut. I called Brother Roloff and told him my plight. Brother Roloff's advice was that I not go the medical route but rather change my diet. He encouraged me to simply change my diet from the meat-based, sugar dessert, Standard American Diet (SAD) I had been consuming the past 42 years of my life and start eating God's original diet as set forth in Genesis 1:29 of the Bible.

And so, in 1976, overnight, I changed my diet from the way I had been eating for the past forty-two years and started eating exclusively raw fruits and vegetables, along with drinking one to two quarts of carrot juice each day. Almost immediately I started to feel better, and within one year, my baseball-sized tumor had disappeared. But not only had my tumor disappeared, so had every other physical problem I had been experiencing; including hypoglycemia, hemorrhoids, severe allergies, sinus problems, high blood pressure, fatigue, and pimple outbreaks. Why, even my dandruff and body odor were gone in less than twelve months.

At the end of that first year I did modify my diet to include some cooked food again—adding back such items as baked white and sweet potatoes, brown rice and other cooked grains, steamed vegetables, baked squash, and some whole-grain pasta. It has now been well over 20 years since making that initial diet change from the world's SAD diet to God's Genesis 1:29 diet. In the 20 plus years since I stopped nourishing my body according to the world's dictates, I have not experienced as much as a cold, sore throat, headache, or upset stomach, and I haven't been to a doctor or taken as much as an aspirin. Hallelujah!

In January of 1991, Rhonda (who is now my wife) attended a Health Seminar I was giving in Rogersville, Tennessee. At that time, she had severe rheumatoid arthritis and was very overweight. Her arthritis was so bad she couldn't turn her head more than an inch in either direction. She couldn't walk a block without extreme pain and difficulty, and, at times, was taking as many as four to six ibuprofen an hour for that pain. Within one year from the time she adopted the Hallelujah Diet, she had lost 85 pounds in weight, dropped from a size 20 dress to a 12, was speed walking four miles each morning without pain, and all her arthritis problems were gone. Another Hallelujah!

Because of the tremendous physical healing we both had experienced, in 1992, Rhonda and I started Hallelujah Acres, a ministry to help Christians appreciate and to better understand their beautiful physical bodies, and to also realize there is a better way of dealing with physical problems than the way we have always been taught. At Hallelujah Acres, we teach health from a Biblical perspective. The ministry has grown extremely rapidly and today we estimate we have over a million people around the world following our program in some form while tens of thousands have written or called to tell us that they experienced similar healing within their bodies when they followed our teachings.

My purpose in writing this Primer

The purpose of this 'primer' is to share with the Christian community what I have learned in the more than 20 years since I changed my diet and started researching how diet and lifestyle affects our health. It is my prayer that this little book will be a help and blessing to all who read it. Please read it and re-read it with an open mind and please do not judge its contents until you have searched the Scriptures, investigated the most cutting edge scientific knowledge, and given our program at least a 21-day evaluation in your own body.

You Don't Have to Be Sick

"Beloved, I wish above all things that thou mayest prosper and be in health, even as thy soul prospereth" (3 John 2).

Are you aware that today, in modern America, as we enter the 21st Century, over nine out of every ten people reading this book will die from a disease?

Half will die from a heart attack or stroke. Three or more will die from cancer. Most of the rest will die from complications associated with diabetes, asthma, arthritis, Alzheimer's, AIDs, or a host of other diseases.

The drugs the doctors use offer little help and, unfortunately, in most cases, make people even sicker. Ironically, the doctors are as sick as their patients, experiencing the same physical problems and suffering from the same diseases.

The medical community is obsessed with curing disease and constantly promises that if we give them enough money and enough time, they will find a cure for everything that ails us.

Well, they have had a lot of money and a lot of time.

But they still have no cure for cancer, heart disease, diabetes, arthritis, AIDs, or even the common cold.

The cost of so-called health care continues to rise alarmingly with each passing day. Current annual health care costs, in America alone, stands at over one trillion dollars and rising.

At the same time, the health of the American people continues to deteriorate alarmingly with each passing year.

The diseases we used to consider old age diseases have become our children's diseases. We now have childhood diabetes and childhood arthritis, while cancer has become the number one killer of our youth.

Today, the average four-year-old already has plaque build up in his/her arteries, while over 90% of the youth of America cannot pass the president's minimum physical fitness requirements.

Today, some schools have Ritalin breaks so children can be administered this potent drug right in the schoolhouse, and most schools now have nurses on staff.

During the past hundred years, there has been an explosion of technological advances in this world. We can now fly around the globe at speeds faster than that of sound. We watch pictures of things happening any place on earth as they occur. We can fly to the moon and send explorer satellites into space.

Yet in the area of disease and health care, we are literally sicker than our ancestors, and we die of more different diseases than people did a hundred years ago. Why?

- Why, with all the university scientists receiving billions in grant dollars to find cures?
- Why, with all the Foundations and Societies (Cancer, Heart, Diabetes, Arthritis, etc.) raising money to find cures?
- Why, with more medical doctors per capita in America than any other country on earth?

Why are Americans among the sickest people on earth?

Believe it or not, there is a very simple explanation to "why" we get sick, as well as a simple and practical way to eliminate almost all diseases from the face of the earth. And we here at Hallelujah Acres have found it.

Not that we are exceptionally intelligent or because we have vast numbers of university degrees. It is just that we could not accept the deteriorating health we were experiencing in our own physical bodies, we were not happy with the results we were getting from the medical community, and so we went searching for answers.

What we found has not only taken away almost all our own physical problems, but when others apply what we have learned, almost every physical problem they are experiencing also goes away.

What we have found is the CAUSE of almost all diseases, along with a way to eliminate these diseases.

We currently estimate that over a million people worldwide have tried the Hallelujah Diet. And we literally have tens of thousands of testimonies from those who have applied our teachings and who have seen their physical problems simply go away, just like ours went away.

In fact, most people report that over 90% of all physical problems are gone from their bodies in six months or less from the time they adopt the Hallelujah Diet.

Following is an example of the type of letters and e-mails that come into Hallelujah Acres on a daily basis:

My name is Marilyn, and in two months on the Hallelujah Diet I have lost 43 pounds. My blood pressure has lowered from a high of 240/110 to daily readings of around 92/62. Pulse that used to be 110 to 113 at rest now is in the 70's.

My ulcerative colitis is a thing of the past. No more congestive heart failure. I can drive, do housework, shop, take a walk, play with my grandchildren and just live life as I used to after three years of almost being a total bed patient.

I am off all medications. I was on eighteen different medications. My mind is alert and I am so peaceful. Life is such a positive experience.

Puscular psoriasis, which was a life-threatening disease for me is 98% cleared from my skin. I am so thankful for the Hallelujah Diet and what it has accomplished in my life.

I have my life back after being told by doctors I had only a short time left. When I refused to accept that, they told me I was in denial. I knew in God's word he promised me health, I just didn't know how to claim it. The Hallelujah Diet showed me how.

Thank you Rev. Malkmus, and all the wonderful Health Ministers who hold forth this life-giving message from God's Word.

Have you ever asked yourself, WHY do people get sick? Or, WHY are Christians just as sick as non-Christians?

My friend, the answer to both of these questions can be very readily found. You see, there are two systems at work in this world—the world's system and God's system, and when it comes to feeding and taking care of the physical body almost 100% of the people in this world follow the world's system. And yes, that includes most of the Christian community.

The Bible says: *"Know ye not that ye are [your physical body is] the temple of God, and that the Spirit of God dwelleth in you? If any man defile the temple of God [puts something into the body that will harm it], him shall God destroy; for the temple of God is holy, which temple ye are. Let no man deceive himself. If any man among you seemeth to be wise in this world, let him become a fool, that he may be wise. For the wisdom of this world is foolishness with God"* (1 Corinthians 3:16-19).

Sickness and disease are simply our beautiful, God-made bodies reacting to the bad things we are exposing them to. *"Be not deceived; God is not mocked, For whatsoever a man soweth, that shall he also reap"* (Galatians 6:7).

For example, compare our automobiles, designed by men, with our physical bodies, which were designed by God. The creator of the automobile designed his creation to be fueled with a specific type of fuel, and we wouldn't think of putting into the fuel tank of our automobile the wrong fuel or contaminated fuel.

Yet we pay practically no attention to the grade of fuel, or contaminates contained therein, when it comes to what we put into our beautiful, God-made bodies.

The fuel God designed our physical bodies to be nourished with was given to us by God at the time He created man.

What does the Bible tell us that fuel should be? *"And God said, Behold, I have given you every herb [vegetable] bearing seed, which is upon the face of all the earth, and every tree in the which is the fruit of a tree yielding seed; to you it shall be for meat"* (Genesis 1:29).

And we know that these vegetables and fruits were consumed in a natural, raw, organic, uncooked form, because there were no pollutants in the atmosphere and fire had not yet been discovered.

Now compare the diet God originally gave to mankind in Genesis 1:29 with the diet the average American and the average Christian consumes today.

When we enter our modern supermarkets, almost everything on the shelves comes from the food merchants of this world—not from God's garden. In fact, once you leave the fresh fruit and vegetable department in your supermarket and start down all those aisles loaded with cans, jars, boxes, and packages you are literally in the manufactured or dead food section of the store.

Why do Christians get sick?

This is a very easy question to answer. Christians get sick for the same reasons non-Christians get sick—they are putting the wrong fuel (food) into their physical bodies. You see, almost every physical problem we experience is merely the body reacting to our putting into it something God never intended to enter it.

Today most Christians know more about their automobile and the fuel it was designed to run on than they do about their beautiful God-made bodies. For instance, if we put a low-grade fuel in the gas tank of our automobile, it will ping and knock. And if we put a low-grade fuel in our physical bodies we too will ping and knock. Let me give you some physical problems that are simply the body responding to low-grade or contaminated fuel (food).

A very young child may experience colic, ear and throat infections, allergies, asthma, diaper rash, etc. These are all the result of mother putting the wrong fuel (foods) into the child's body. Why, a mother can be nourishing a child at her breast and if she eats the wrong foods, the toxins can pass through the breast milk, enter the baby, and create physical problems.

As we grow older and continue putting the wrong fuel into our bodies, the pinging and knocking progressively becomes louder. Maybe we start gaining excessive weight, have to start wearing eyeglasses, or experience such things as arthritic pain, hypoglycemia, high blood pressure, or the like. These physical problems are all unnecessary pinging and knocking caused by putting the wrong fuel into our bodies. And if we keep putting the wrong fuel into our bodies long enough, it ultimately results in a life-threatening heart attack, stroke, cancer, or death. Heart attacks, strokes, and cancer alone account for the deaths of over 80% of all Christians. My Christian friend, almost every one of the physical problems just mentioned are caused by our putting the wrong fuel (foods) into our bodies and/or by living the wrong lifestyle.

If we want to start living in health rather than sickness, we must change what we eat. We must change from eating the world's foods to God's foods. We must start doing things God's way. We must start eating and living healthy.

When we make this simple diet and lifestyle change from the world's diet to God's diet, usually within six months or less (and usually much less), ninety plus percent of all physical problems will be gone and sickness will probably never visit our body again. And this is no pie-in-the-sky statement. We have tens of thousands who have personally experienced this self-healing and know it to be true and are today rejoicing in superior health.

Romans 12:1-2 says, *"I beseech you therefore, brethren, by the mercies of God, that ye present your bodies a living sacrifice, holy, acceptable unto God, which is your reasonable service. And be not conformed to this world..."*

Christians get sick because they have conformed to the diet and lifestyle of this world.

Christians eat in the same fast food restaurants and consume the same junk foods as the world community. Compare the diet of the average Christian with that of the average non-Christian and you will find absolutely no difference in what they eat. Each group eats the same diet, thus creating the same physical problems. Do you realize that the percentage of Christians experiencing cancer, heart attacks and strokes, diabetes, as well as all other physical problems is the same in both the Christian and non-Christian communities?

How do Christians deal with physical problems?

What do non-Christians do when they get sick? Why they run just as fast as they can to the medical doctor. **What do Christians do when they get sick? They *pray* first, and then run as fast as they can to the same medical doctors as do non-Christians.** And what do medical doctors give Christians? The same drugs and treatments they give non-Christians.

What about drugs?

Christians seem to think that there are two classifications of drugs: 1) Bad drugs, such as, alcohol, nicotine, heroine, and cocaine, etc. and 2) Good drugs, such as, doctor prescribed and over the counter drugs. While doctor-prescribed and over the counter drugs fit into another category and are good. Is there a difference between the drugs the doctors give us and the drugs we preach and teach against in our churches? Not according to the Bible. In Revelations 18:23, the Bible states, *"...for by thy sorceries (drugs) were all nations deceived."* The Biblical word for "sorceries" comes from the Greek word "phar-ma-kia," which in today's English is translated 'drugs.' Thus, the Bible condemns the use of *all* drugs.

Christians fail to realize that doctor-prescribed and over the counter drugs are just as toxic (and sometimes habit forming) as the drugs we teach and preach against in our churches. In fact, many times the doctor's drugs are even more harmful and dangerous than the drugs we teach and preach against.

As I mentioned earlier, in April of 1998 the *Journal of the American Medical Association* reported that over 100,000 Americans die each year from the poisoning effects (side effects) of these doctor-prescribed drugs while over two million have to be hospitalized.

Only when Christians get off the world's diet and get back to God's diet will things improve.

Why does God often not answer our prayers for healing?

Because He placed us in a physical body, on a physical earth and created these physical bodies to be governed by His natural physical laws. Just as a Christian cannot escape the penalty for violating the law of gravity, neither can he escape the natural laws God established as to what is and what is not proper fuel or food for the physical body. Now, God can do anything, and He certainly can overrule the physical laws of nature that He established. But when we look at our churches and see that the physical problems being experienced in the Christian community today are identical in volume and intensity to the non-Christian community—we must acknowledge that something is seriously wrong. If we keep doing what we have always done in the past, we will continue to experience the same horrible consequences.

The Christian Community is on the wrong road when it comes to how to nourish and maintain their physical bodies. Christians have somehow placed this beautiful physical body God has provided each of us into the spiritual realm. But we do not possess a spiritual body. We possess a physical body. When we become Christians, the spiritual enters into our physical bodies (in the person of the Holy Spirit) through a new birth experience, but the body itself remains a physical entity. (See John 3:3; 1 Corinthians 6:19-20; and 1 Corinthians 3:26-17).

Because of this misunderstanding, Christians think that all they have to do is pray a spiritual prayer before they put physical food into their physical body, and that somehow that spiritual prayer will remove the physical cholesterol and its effect on the physical body. My dear Christian friend, it just doesn't work that way. We are reaping exactly what we have been sowing.

"Be not deceived, God is not mocked; for whatsoever a man soweth, that shall he also reap." And, *"My people are destroyed for lack of knowledge..."* (Galatians 6:7 and Hosea 4:6)

Often, Christians approach me at seminars or write or call, and they are literally angry at God because of a physical problem that did not go away after they had prayed for healing. These people fail to realize that the physical problem they are experiencing was created by themselves, and that God will usually not restore health to the physical body when it is self-inflicted by improper diet and lifestyle.

Does God want Christians to be sick?

Of course not. Listen as the Bible answers this question in 3 John 2, *"Beloved, I wish above all things that thou mayest prosper and be in health, even as thy soul prospereth."*

No, God did not make a mistake when He created man, nor did He create man to die from heart attacks, strokes, cancer, diabetes, and the like. In fact, most of these diseases were not even known to mankind until fairly recent years. These are man-made diseases—*not* God made.

When we get sick, we must not blame that sickness on God. When we get sick, we are simply reaping what we have been sowing.

Where did sickness originate?

In my early Christian life, I was taught that sickness originated with the fall of man in the garden, and that sickness was a part of the curse God placed upon man as a result of Adam's sin and disobedience. And yet, as I study my Bible, I do not find any mention of physical illness occurring for almost 2,000 years after the fall. In fact, the Bible reveals that in the period of history between the fall and the flood, man lived an average of 912 years without a single recorded instance of sickness.

Then comes chapter 6 in the book of Genesis where we find God very upset with man. Why was God so angry?

"And God saw that the wickedness of man was great in the earth, and that every imagination of the thoughts of his heart was only evil continually. And it repented the Lord that he had made man on the earth, and it grieved him at his heart. And the Lord said, I will destroy man whom I have created from the face of the earth... But Noah found grace in the eyes of the Lord." (Genesis 6:5-8)

In Genesis 6:12 we find that God was not only upset with man because of his wickedness, but also because *"...all flesh had corrupted (God's) way upon the earth."* In other words, God was not only angry with man because of sin, but also because man had changed the way God wanted man to live. And that is exactly what we have done in our Christian communities today regarding the physical body. In terms of that which pertains to our physical bodies we have totally left God and His ways and adapted the ways of the world.

As we said earlier, we eat the world's diet, suffer the world's ills, go to the world's doctors, take the world's drugs, and experience the same consequences in our physical bodies as does the non-Christian community.

How did man's diet evolve?

In Chapters 1 and 2 of the Bible we read how God created man, placed him in a garden setting and in Genesis 1:29 told man what he was supposed to eat.

Clearly, God intended man to forage for his food as found naturally in nature, and thus his diet was to consist solely of the raw fruits and vegetables as found in nature. We also know that this original diet did not include grains because man had no way of harvesting or cooking them. Fire had not yet been discovered, and there is no evidence that man cooked his food prior to the flood. And this original diet did not include animal flesh as clearly brought out in the latter part of Genesis 1:29. So all Biblical evidence points to man being sustained on a pure raw fruit and vegetable diet prior to the flood in Genesis 7.

Immediately after the flood, however, in Genesis 9:3, God says something that appears to be a contradictory statement. Listen to what He says. *"Every moving thing that liveth shall be meat for you, even as the green herb have I given you all things."* (Compare this verse with Genesis 1:29.)

Why did God allow meat to be added to the diet?

After almost two thousand years on a raw vegetable and fruit diet, WHY did God allow man, whom He created to be vegetarian, to put the flesh of an animal into his/her body? There have been a number of theories advanced:

1. One theory is that all the earth had been covered with water by the flood, destroying all plant life, and thus flesh was all that was available (from the animals in the ark).

2. Another explanation involves the 'canopy theory,' which teaches that the earth was enveloped by a huge greenhouse prior to the flood and its removal somehow caused a change in man's diet.

3. My theory is different, however, and please remember that this is only my theory. I personally believe that God used the consuming of animal flesh to shorten the life span of man. Let me share my thoughts:

In Genesis, chapters five and six, we see that God was not very happy with man—in fact so unhappy, God was threatening to wipe out the entire human race. And if it had not been for Noah, none of us would be here today. So in these chapters we see God threatening to destroy the entire human race, then changing His mind because of Noah, and then saying that He is going to destroy only those who did not heed Noah's warning of the impending flood. Thus the human race would be spared.

In Genesis 6:3, we find God making a very interesting statement: ***"...My spirit shall not always strive with man, for that he also is flesh: yet his days shall be an hundred and twenty years."*** I find this statement very important in light of the fact that God originally created man to live forever (Genesis 3:22). And even after the fall, on God's original raw fruit and vegetable diet, man lived an average of 912 years in a physical body just like yours and mine.

Why did God shorten man's life span?

My theory is that man was living so long on planet earth (because of the raw fruit and vegetable diet) and getting into so much trouble because of that long life that God chose to reduce the length of each individual's life, rather than destroy the entire human race. So God allows the human race to continue, but uses a natural means (the consuming of animal flesh) to shorten the life span.

Does the Bible support this theory?

To Biblically substantiate this theory, you will note that just as soon as man started to consume the flesh of animals, his life span started to drop dramatically. From an average of 912 years (the life span on raw fruits and vegetables before the flood) to 110 years in ten generations after the introduction of animal flesh. (See Genesis 50:26).

What about Peter's Vision in Acts 10?

In this portion of Scripture, I do not believe God was commanding Peter to go out and kill and eat those animals God had forbidden His people in the Old Testament. Rather, as this portion of Scripture is read in its context, the Lord was using the dietary laws of the Old Testament as an illustration so that Peter could understand that he should take the Gospel to the Gentiles. To substantiate this thought, you will find that immediately after Peter saw the vision, Gentiles, who were considered "unclean" by Jewish believers, were knocking at Peter's door, and Peter shared the Gospel with them.

But Jesus himself ate fish!

As for Jesus serving and consuming fish, the only theory I have is that Jesus did not come to change the social structure or diets or lifestyle that existed in that day. Rather, He came to prove who He was, and to shed His precious blood to redeem mankind. Why, Jesus didn't even condemn slavery while He was here, no less seek to change diet and lifestyle!

What about other Bible verses that talk about meat?

There are other verses in the Bible that use the word "meat," and I don't claim to have answers for all of them. However, I do know there are at least 30 verses in the New Testament alone where the translators used the word "meat" when the proper translation should have been "food," "act of eating," "anything to eat," "table," or "nourishment." In other words, the translators, in translating the text from Greek to English, used the word "meat" inappropriately. The translators made the same error with the use of the word "wine." When we see the word "wine" in the Bible, it can mean "grape juice" or "pureed grapes" or "fermented wine."

As any concordance will reveal, 1 Timothy 4:3 is a classic example of the improper use of the word "meat" by the translators. Many Christians use 1 Timothy 4:3 to justify their consuming of animal flesh or to condemn those who teach the Genesis 1:29 diet. In actuality, in the Greek language, 1 Timothy 4:3 isn't even talking about animal flesh but instead about certain foods.

Was meat in Bible days different than meat today?

But regardless of how you want to interpret some of the Bible verses pertaining to the subject of meat, the meat being sold today bears no resemblance to meat in Bible days. Meat in Bible days contained three percent fat. Meat today averages twenty to sixty percent fat. Meat in Bible days did not contain the growth hormones and antibiotics and deadly bacteria and other toxic substances that are found in meat today. Did you know that more antibiotics are produced each year for animals than for humans? Meat animals in Bible days grazed on pasture grasses, while meat animals today are fed huge amounts of grain to make them fat. According to a 1997 *U.S. News* article, various "by-products" that include chicken manure, dead cats and dogs, and even rendered (boiled down) road kill are now used as feed. When people eat the flesh of animals grown on these substances, they need to realize the horrible consequences to their beautiful, God-made bodies. Can our bodies grow healthy cells by eating the "meat" of animals fed on chicken manure and the boiled down corpses of other animals? I think not.

Why are animal products so harmful?

If you were to study the anatomy of man, you would find that there is nothing in the physical make-up of man's body to indicate God designed him to be carnivorous.

Man's teeth were not designed to rip and tear flesh. Hydrochloric acid in the human body is too weak to break flesh down. And the digestive system is too long with too many bends and pockets and loops. Simply put, flesh putrefies when placed into the human body.

Today, because of the graining of animals and the addition of antibiotics and hormones, the average person who consumes animal products has a serious physical problem by the age of 40. Sadly, the average child who consumes animal products (flesh and/or dairy) already has plaque build up in his/her arteries by the age of four.

Personally, I have consumed virtually nothing that comes from an animal source in over 20 years, and, no, I do not have any indication of an iron or calcium or B12 or protein deficiency. Nor do I know anyone else whose diet is primarily raw fruits and vegetables who has any indication of a deficiency. Nor do I believe that those who lived prior to the flood, to an average age of 912, had any deficiency on God's raw fruit and vegetable diet.

Isn't it interesting that the more the world's experts tell us how we should take care of our physical bodies, the sicker we become? These experts tell us we need to eat animal products for protein and calcium and B12, but they don't warn us of the dangers of animal products. Nor do most of them warn us of the dangers of sugar, salt, white flour, caffeine, hydrogenated fats, etc.

If we want to experience true physical health, not only do we need to start putting nutritious foods into our bodies, but we must also stop putting in the bad foods.

What must we do to turn things around?

Knowledge and reprogramming are the keys. The Bible states in John 8:32, *"And ye shall know the truth, and the truth shall make you free."*

Knowledge comes by exposing our minds to truth and then as we act on these truths, we are set free. Re-read Romans 12:1-2.

Just as our forefathers declared their independence from England in 1776, we, as Christians, must declare our independence from the world's system that has enslaved our physical bodies for so long.

We can declare our independence by eating LIVING food!

You see, God provided each of us with an incredible, *living*, physical body. Each of our bodies is comprised of approximately one hundred trillion *living* cells.

These *living* cells were designed by God to be nourished *exclusively* with *living* (*raw*) *food*. All cooked food (including items that come in a can, jar, box, bottle, or container of any kind) is *dead food*. You see, for foods to have a long shelf life and not spoil, and make the food merchants lots of money, the *life force* (enzymes) must be destroyed.

God says, *"I have set before you life and death, blessing and cursing: therefore choose life, that both thou and thy seed may live"* (Deuteronomy 30:19).

If you were to take a *living* (raw) carrot, cut off its top, and place it in a saucer of water, it would grow and produce new green leaves. But if you cooked that carrot and then cut off the top and put it into a saucer of water you would find that it would no longer grow. Why? It is now dead because we destroyed the *life force* within that carrot with the heat.

Another illustration is to take a newborn baby cow and allow it to nurse at the mother cow. If we did that, the calf would grow into a strong, healthy animal.

But, if immediately upon birth, that calf was removed from its mother and fed exclusively pasteurized (cooked) milk, the calf would be dead in less than 60 days.

Why? Because God created cows as well as all other forms of animal life (including man) to be nourished with *living* food. Every creature in the animal kingdom was designed by God to be nourished exclusively with living, raw food, and man is the only member to alter God's design and plan.

To attain ultimate health, you need to give up the five foods that are killing you.

With the idea of living food in mind, let's examine the diet of the average American and the average Christian. What do we find? We find that well over 90% of everything consumed as food in America today has been cooked. This cooking destroys all enzymes (the life force within plants); destroys a high percentage of the vitamins; converts protein to uric acid; and changes the organic (living) minerals into an inorganic or dead form. In addition,

Animal products are loaded with fat. In one year the average American meat eater puts into his/her body over 100 pounds of fat. This fat enters the bloodstream and builds up on the artery walls, causing the heart to work harder in an effort to pump the blood through the crud, thus elevating blood pressure and ultimately causing one-half of all deaths in America due to heart attacks and strokes. Margarines and other hydrogenated oils do the same thing.

At Hallelujah Acres, we teach that

- If we eliminate animal products, margarine, and other hydrogenated oils from our diets, we will reduce our risk of ever having a heart attack or stroke by 96%.
- If we do not smoke or consume animal products or take estrogen, we would reduce our risk of cancer to almost zero.
- If we eliminate these animal fats and hydrogenated oils from our diet, we would reduce the risk of developing adult-onset diabetes to almost zero.
- If we eliminate the animal products from our diets, we would reduce our risk of osteoporosis to almost zero.
- Eliminating animal products from our diet will also eliminate almost all colon problems, and most acid stomach problems will disappear in less than a week.

Cow milk was designed by God to nourish a 50 to 90 pound baby cow at birth and nourish it until it was old enough to eat grass on its own. The protein content of cow's milk is many times higher than human mother's breast milk and has a totally different chemical composition. When cow milk is placed into a human baby, it often causes colic, all kinds of mucus membrane problems, allergies, asthma, and even diaper rashes.

And when you look at the ingredients in infant formulas and compare the ingredients with human mother's breast milk, you find the formulas severely lacking. Also, formulas are devoid of enzymes, the life force. Watch what often happens to a child when mother switches the child from her breast to formula. Usually the body reacts with runny noses, fevers, and often the child is put on medication. In reality, the runny nose and fever are nothing but the body reacting to the wrong fuel.

Sugar is an immune system suppressant. God gave us an immune system to protect the health and integrity of our beautiful bodies. When we consume concentrated amounts of sugar, we short-circuit our immune system and prevent it from doing its job. At the beginning of the 20th Century, the average American consumed seven pounds of sugar per year. Today, each individual in America consumes some 150 pounds. This breaks down to over 50 teaspoons *per day*. (On average, a 12-oz can of soda pop contains 11 teaspoons of sugar; ice cream is about 37% sugar; while most breakfast cereals contain over 50% sugar.) In addition to compromising our immune system, we teach that sugar affects our emotions, contributing to depression in adults and Attention Deficit Disorders in children and teenagers.

Table salt and all minerals originating in the earth or ocean or found in mineral supplements are in a dead form and thus toxic to the body. These inorganic minerals contribute to kidney stones and gall stones. Plaque and hardening of the arteries result when these minerals join with the fat in our bodies.

White flour is devoid of fiber and contains zero nutrition. Yes, the chemists who create our "food" these days do add coal-tar vitamins back in after processing, but these aren't natural, real vitamins. We teach that the vitamins added to manufactured foods are in the wrong form and thus toxic to the body.

All five of the above listed, so-called foods, have one thing in common—they contain *no fiber*. Because the American people are consuming a diet that is almost totally devoid of fiber, some 70% of the American people suffer from constipation problems.

You'll feel better without caffeine and growth hormones in your body.

Caffeine, as found in coffee, tea, chocolate, and most soft drinks is an addictive drug. We teach that caffeine damages the lining of our stomachs, constricts arteries, contributes to heart attacks and strokes, damages liver and kidneys, and may contribute to at least six different kinds of cancers.

Estrogen in these animal products, in our opinion, is also jump-starting puberty in our children. Fifty years ago, most girls experienced puberty after the age of 15. Following World War II, the meat industry began putting synthetic hormones into animals and animal feed to hasten growth. More recently, the dairy industry started using hormones so cows would produce larger quantities of milk.

After 50 years of consuming these hormones, the age of puberty has plunged to ages 8, 9, and 10.

At Hallelujah Acres we teach that growth hormones (estrogen), as found in animal products, and the estrogen being prescribed by medical doctors may well be the primary cause of most breast, uterine, and prostate cancers.

Someone reading this treatise may ask, "Do you have any valid, scientific documentation for all these wild claims you have been making?" The answer is an emphatic "Yes!" And I will share several of them with you.

Dr. Pottenger's research of raw versus cooked.

One of the best-known studies of raw versus cooked foods involves a 10-year research project conducted by Dr. Francis M. Pottenger, using hundreds of cats. His study was published in 1946 in the *American Journal of Orthodontics and Oral Surgery*. Dr. Pottenger fed all the cats the same food, with the only difference being that one group received it raw, while the others received it cooked.

The results dramatically revealed the advantages of raw foods over a cooked diet. Cats that were fed raw, living food produced healthy kittens year after year with no ill health or premature death. But cats fed the same food, only cooked, developed heart disease, cancer, kidney and thyroid disease, pneumonia, paralysis, loss of teeth, arthritis, birthing difficulties, diminished sexual interest, diarrhea, irritability, liver problems, osteoporosis, and more (the same diseases common in our human cooked–food culture).

The first generation of kittens, from cats fed cooked food, were sick and abnormal, the second generation were often born diseased or dead, and by the third generation, the mothers were sterile.

Rural Chinese are healthier because they eat natural foods.

The second scientific documentation I want to mention can be found summarized in a book entitled *The China Project*. This is a Cornell-based scientific study of the most comprehensive survey ever conducted of the relationship between diet and disease. The study was conducted in rural China during the 1980's. The location of the study is of major importance because entire villages in rural China eat the same locally grown food for their entire lives, unlike in the West where food from all around the world is available.

Availability of specific types of food varies considerably throughout rural China, so researchers were able to detect obvious links between diet and specific diseases as over 1,000 pieces of information were taken from each of over 10,000 people. "One of the most dramatic findings...was the strong association between foods of animal origin and cancer," the book states.

High cholesterol from animal products and high urea nitrogen from excessive protein in animal products were related to increased rates of heart disease, leukemia, and cancer;

"...only small intakes of animal products were associated with significant increases in chronic degenerative diseases. And even more exciting, that the greater the percentage of plant food in our diet, the less chance of getting these diseases."

Another factor directly associated with breast cancer is the young age of puberty in America. "Chinese girls reach menstruation usually when they are 15 to 19 years old."

With acceptance of a vegetarian diet and elimination of recreational drugs and improved sanitation, *The China Project* concludes: "Scientists estimate that premature deaths from all diseases could be reduced by 80 to 90%."

Listen to what God has to say about all this.

"I beseech you therefore, brethren, by the mercies of God, that ye present your bodies a living sacrifice, holy, acceptable unto God, which is your reasonable service. And be not conformed to this world: but be ye transformed by the renewing of your mind, that ye may prove what is that good, and acceptable, and perfect, will of God" (Romans 12:1–2).

How do we renew (reprogram) our minds?

The very first thing we must do to change programming is realize that our current programming came from the world's system and not from God. We must realize that the experts we have been looking to for answers regarding nourishing our bodies and dealing with physical breakdown came from this worldly system, and that these experts were simply imparting to us what they had been taught in the world's universities.

For example, all that is needed to become an expert is to earn a degree in one of these universities. To earn that degree, all that is required is to take the required courses in the subject you want a degree in and then agree with what you are taught sufficiently to receive passing grades and ultimately a degree or doctorate in that subject. But the question we never think to ask is: "What if what they are teaching in these universities is *not truth*?"

Do licensed dieticians actually know anything about human nutrition?

Here is what I am getting at—all meals served in our school lunch programs must be approved by registered dietitians. To become a dietitian, a person must hold a degree from a college or university. This degree supposedly qualifies dieticians to know what good nutrition is so they can teach others and watch over the ignorant populace (those who haven't taken these classes and received these degrees).

But what are these experts teaching us, and what are they feeding our children? Check up on the lunches being served in your local school and you will probably find them serving hot dogs, cheeseburgers, French fries, and pizza, along with soft drinks, pasteurized milk and sugar desserts, as well as a host of other toxic substances. These are not real foods. Rather, they are manufactured, non-food substances of this world's system, which cause our children's bodies to break down. These dietician-approved "foods" ultimately lead to sickness and disease.

You can find another example of the ignorance being displayed by these experts by taking a good look at the meals being served sick people in the hospitals. If a person knows anything at all about this physical body and how it was designed by God to be nourished, he would realize that institutional meals appear to be designed to keep people sick and in the hospital rather than helping them to get well so they could go home.

Now look at the medical doctors, trained in these same worldly universities, and you will find that they are being taught to deal with the symptoms of disease rather than the causes of disease.

So the doctors poison our bodies with drugs, burn our bodies with radiation, and mutilate our bodies with surgeries. Then, when this worldly system fails to provide healing, we are told to get ready to die. How tragic.

Sadly, the Christian Community is being just as deceived by this world's system as is the non-Christian Community.

So even though the Bible condemns this world's system and this world's way of nourishing and taking care of these marvelous physical bodies, the average Christian follows the world's experts instead of God's ways as set forth in the Bible. Sadly, many of the universities that are today teaching the world's way were once bastions for Biblical truth.

But they have been taken over by the world's intellectuals and now teach the world's system rather than God's. When young Christians attend these worldly universities, they are often intimidated and ridiculed by these intellectuals and consequently alter their views on creation and other Biblical teachings. Christians often forget the Bible's warnings concerning wisdom:

"Let no man deceive himself. If any man among you seemeth to be wise in this world, let him become a fool, that he may be wise. For the wisdom of this world is foolishness with God." "If any of you lack wisdom, let him ask of God..." (1 Corinthians 3:18-19 and James 1:5).

Preachers occasionally accuse me of putting too much emphasis on the physical body. Yet the Bible is full of verses pertaining to the physical body and telling of our need to properly care for it:

"What? Know ye not that your BODY is the temple of the Holy Ghost which is in you, which ye have of God, and ye are not your own? For ye are bought with a price: therefore glorify God in your BODY, and in your spirit, which are God's" (1 Corinthians 6:20).

"...and I pray God your whole spirit and soul and BODY be preserved blameless unto the coming of our Lord Jesus Christ" (I Thessalonians 5:23).

"Some may retort that the work of winning souls is more important than helping people stay or get well physically or than prolonging their lives. But unless men who know the Word of God and who have the riches of experience stay well and alive physically, how can they tell the message of man's redemption?" (Quoted from *God's Key to Health and Happiness*, by Elmer A. Josephson, a Baptist Minister).

In an open letter to Hillary Clinton in January 1994, I wrote:

"…Our present health-care system is geared to provide what is most profitable for physicians, drug companies, and hospitals, not to what is best for the people of our great land. This, Mrs. Clinton, is what must be changed if you and your husband wish to implement true health care reform. If the health of the American people is to be improved and if the staggering cost of health care is to be curbed, we must look outside the current and established systems.

"And I am not advocating the use of synthetic vitamins, herbs, or homeopathic remedies as the solution. These substances, along with all drugs, only deal with symptoms caused by improper diet and lifestyle.

"What I am saying is that almost all physical problems are caused by putting into our bodies substances that they were never biologically designed to handle… substances that are actually toxic to the body.

"Almost all physical problems can be eliminated and perfect health can be maintained by proper diet and lifestyle."

Some final thoughts

God placed us on a magnificently beautiful earth in a gorgeous garden over which we were to be caretakers. But we have left that garden and are raping the land God gave us as an inheritance.

We humans have been gradually destroying our planet, using up its resources. Destroying our forests. Polluting our air and water. Building ever more hospitals and prisons.

While all too many of the American people seem to be interested in is how much money they can make and how many material possessions and physical comforts they can obtain.

With all of this technology and money and material possessions and comforts—*we have forgotten God!* We are also a nation made up of people who are starving to death on full stomachs.

We are a nation of sick people, and we watch even those with abundant wealth, political position, and great worldly knowledge die of the same diseases as those we consider less fortunate.

It does not display great intelligence to make a fortune only to lose one's health and die of a heart attack or stroke or cancer.

Most diseases are avoidable, and the ever increasing degree of sickness only reflects the ignorance of our supposedly well-informed leaders and medical technocrats, together with the money-making aspirations of the food manufacturers and the pharmaceutical industry.

If we are to turn this whole thing around and bring healing to ourselves and to our brothers and sisters, we must turn from the world's way back to God's way.

We here at Hallelujah Acres have done just that and are experiencing abundant health while we serve our wonderful God and Saviour, Jesus Christ.

Won't you join us?

Some Typical Testimonies of Healing

May I share with you a few testimonies of those who have regained their health by living God's way instead of man's way?

From a man with bone cancer

"Dear Rev. Malkmus:

On June 30, 1997, I was diagnosed with Multiple Myeloma, bone marrow cancer... The day the doctor told us of the cancer, I asked him about diet. He said, 'It doesn't matter what you eat.'

That did not set well with me. I asked two other doctors the same question and received the same answer. I decided I was going to make some changes anyway.

In July, our son's girlfriend, who had cervical cancer, came by to visit and brought ten issues of Back to the Garden, dating back to 1993. They were 'eye opening'...

By the way, our son's girlfriend who went on the Hallelujah Diet has been given a clean bill of health...

On November 3, they took a bone marrow biopsy and on the morning of the seventh I received the results. I am cancer free. Praise God.

While the doctors tell me the disease is incurable and will probably return in two to four years, I choose to believe the report of the Lord. He has an ultimate way to health (both spiritual and physical) that is by-and-large rejected by our culture today."

—Tom Wadsworth

From a singer with back problems

"... I am a great fan of Rev. Malkmus and about a year ago I went on his diet and changed my life... a year ago I was crippled to the point of pulling myself out of bed each morning on a wire after hurting my back two years prior... then I learned of the Hallelujah Diet. After three weeks on the program, I was bouncing out of bed like a 16-year old. I am a professional Christian Country Singer from Nashville..."

—Steve Hamby

From a woman with a host of illnesses

"I have been on the Hallelujah Diet for four months. I have lost 22 pounds, and I feel great. Before this diet change, I was suffering from Chronic Fatigue Syndrome, headaches, severe stomach problems, hemorrhoids, rectal bleeding, blurred vision, dizziness, sinus problems, and flu-like symptoms. Thanks to your diet—I feel GREAT."

—Karen Brooks

From a lady suffering with fibromyalgia

"I don't know where to begin as to what God has done in my life. I suffer from what the doctor calls fibromyalgia. I also have disc problems. I began the

Hallelujah Diet a month ago. At the time I started I was taking seven different prescriptions, including one with codeine.

In the past few years I have been unable to clean the house or care for my family the way I would like. This past year I have been forced to use a cane.

That is all in the past because since going on the Hallelujah Diet I clean my own home. Am able to stand and cook at the end of the day instead of putting up my swollen legs.

I am no longer taking two of my pain medications, and for the first time in a year I am not taking any codeine.

I thank my Heavenly Father for showing such loving care for me and bringing this diet to my attention. It is proof once more that the Bible is the one and only and final authority."

—Barbara and Charles Shoemaker

From a man with acid stomach

"I had just been told by a medical doctor that I would have to take medicine for my acid stomach problems for the rest of my life. Then I read the Hallelujah plan and decided to make a drastic change. I have had no stomach problems since going on your diet."

—Rinaldo Rocquin, Moscow, Russia

From a woman who refused chemotherapy

"Last December a tumor in my left breast was diagnosed as malignant. In January it was surgically removed. In follow-up, the oncologist prescribed a very strong regimen of chemotherapy and radiation. I told him I needed to go home and pray about it. He said, 'Woman, you do not have time to pray.' His attitude was simply too strong for me. I just felt intuitively that I could not put my life into his hands. I left knowing God would help me find the answer. He did. My nephew told me about your program. I have been on the Hallelujah Diet since February and my general condition is very good. Thanks Rev. Malkmus for paving the way for so many of us..."

—Hazel Eldon

From a medical doctor

"Dear Pastor Malkmus:

I am writing to express my gratefulness to you for what God has done through the ministry of Hallelujah Acres. Two years ago a dear friend gave me a book to read titled Why Christians Get Sick. I really did not have any interest in knowing why Christians get sick... However, I did start to read the book and after the first few pages quickly and pridefully judged the book as nonsense.

Little did I know that God would use this book to begin a remarkable process in my life that would transform my view of treating chronic illness.

During the first few months God convicted me of my pride and purposed to humbly read Why Christians Get Sick. Praise God for what He has done.

I have since abandoned a traditional approach to medical practice and have turned to treating chronic illness through nutrition...

God has burdened me, as He has you, to share this message with our Christian brothers and sisters. May God continue to bless you as you serve Him."

—Stephen Boyajian, M.D.

From a lady with arthritis

"I have had arthritic fingers and joints for several years. The lumps in my fingers are going down and my rings are loose. I took an arthritic medicine (Feldine) in 1993 and almost died from the blood clots it caused. I was in the hospital 48 straight days and had body parts removed due to this.

Today I feel great on the Hallelujah Diet."

—Elizabeth Vaun

From a woman whose lupus has been healed

"I began the Hallelujah Diet five weeks ago... I have had breast cancer, lupus, asthma, arthritis, etc. I determined God did not desire more doctors and radiation, so by an act of faith I went forward in my church for healing. Someone I didn't know brought me your diet. I read and checked you out and then they gave me the juicer, book, and first jar of Barleygreen.

How could I refuse the Lord? Praise God, in this short time my lupus doctor said I didn't need to go there again unless there was a problem. I am off the lupus medicine.

I am off my daily sinus medicine and have only two more to go. I am already feeling much better and am looking for total healing. Oh, and I don't need to go to my oncologist for a year. Praise God. Thank you so much for caring for so many people."

—Janet Eshelman

From a man with colon cancer

"Marilyn and I are eternally grateful to George's willingness to talk with us in December, 1997, after John learned he had colon cancer via a colonoscopy on November 21, 1997, and a pathology report of eight samples that were all malignant.

After seeking the Lord's guidance and learning of Rev. Malkmus' success in recovering from his colon cancer in 1976 and the success of Health Minister Larry Lerew in doing the same in 1996, we decided to follow the Hallelujah program, and we praise God for the results.

In April 1998, a follow-up colonoscopy with accompanying pathology report of five biopsy samples showed that the mass has changed its biological makeup and is now benign.

The doctor was amazed and said, 'This just doesn't happen.' But it did. We praise God and give him all the credit."

—John and Marilyn Spilker

From a diabetic rejuvenated at age 62

"*Since March I have been on the Hallelujah Diet. The reason I am writing is to tell you how last year my hemoglobin A/C was 10.5 (very high). Last week when I went to the doctor (eight months after going on the Hallelujah Diet) my hemoglobin was 6.1, near normal. The doctor said to the nurse, "She's had diabetes thirty years, has an A/C of 6, and has lost 10 pounds. I'd say she's in top condition.'*

All my other reports were great, and he could not argue with my diet. Praise God. Everyone asks me how I stay so young and healthy looking at 62, and I tell them."

—Donna Williams

From the wife of a man given up for dead

"*My husband was diagnosed with cancer at the end of August, and we were offered no hope. No chemo, no radiation, nothing. Someone loaned us God's Way to Ultimate Health and my husband got straight on the Barleygreen and only raw fruit and vegetables. At mid-February there is no evidence of cancer."*

—Dawn Turner, Australia

From a couple with depression and high blood pressure

"*My wife and I got your book God's Way to Ultimate Health about three weeks ago and started using the information that day. In three weeks my wife has lost 12 pounds and her depression has gotten a lot better. I have lost 23 pounds and my blood pressure has come down enough that my doctor has cut my pill in half and told me if it stays down for the next month she will stop it all together. Thank you so very much for giving us back our lives. You have opened our eyes to God's perfect way..."*

—Gary and Margaret Cobb

From a woman who lost both weight and health problems

"*I started the Hallelujah Diet on January 27, 1998. I have lost a total of 24 pounds; energy level increased; fibromyalgia symptoms gone (taking no medication for the first time in seven years); improved attitude; decreased depression; improved PMS; hiatal hernia symptoms gone; tachycardia symptoms gone; sleep improved; etc.*

I could go on and on...

My mother, a very skeptical nurse, has lowered her cholesterol by 80 points in six weeks, and her blood pressure is normal for the first time in ten years.

My teenage son is like a different child. His acne is greatly improved, but his attitude is incredible. He is quieter and more helpful and respectful."

—Christie Morgan

From a lady with foot problems

"*I had 'simple surgery' to correct a bunion on my right foot and some cysts on both feet twenty-four years ago. Five surgeries later, I found myself in 'old-lady'* orthopedic shoes that helped the pain, but I was never pain free—even with Tylenol and Motrin every day. Well, when I started on the Hallelujah Diet in July 1996, I had no idea what all it would fix.

Would you believe that I can now wear regular shoes? I have very little pain in my feet, except when I get off the diet and eat meat or dairy."

—Jane

Doctors can't believe their eyes.

"Dear Rev. Malkmus:

Your diet is sweeping the nation. Last January my dad was diagnosed with a rare soft tissue cancer. He visited several hospitals and talked to many specialists. They gave him 5-10 months to live with or without treatments.

Needless to say, he was frightened, along with all of my family. Praise the Lord, someone gave him your tapes to listen to... Everything you said made so much sense to him he started on your program right away.

About a month or two later, another specialist told him he was going to remove a portion of his right side, near the rib cage, where they had previously found the cancer, just to see if maybe they could remove all the cancer before it spread.

Well, they did the surgery (leaving a huge crater in his side), tested 80 samples of tissue, and were surprised to see that there was NO CANCER.

Through your diet and many hours of prayer, my dad today is cancer free. Thank you for your ministry. I stand behind what you say, and I know my family does too. God's way is truly the right way."

—Chris Goodman

From a medical student

Dear Rev. Malkmus:

I would like to formally thank you for all that you have done for my family, myself, and all of God's people...

I am a graduate student in the department of Cell and Molecular Pharmacology and Experimental Therapeutics at a medical university.

I have been doing what you refer to as the Hallelujah Diet for over a year now—to the extreme—totally raw... I have realized the power and full potential of this truth.

This is the cure to cancer, heart disease, diabetes, and almost every disease...

—Tobiah Pettus

From a research scientist

"Dear Rev. Malkmus:

I have reviewed your teaching series on Back to the Garden and the success that you have had with your modified raw diet. The tape lectures that I have reviewed were inspiring to me.

I am a research scientist retired from the FDA/NIH (Food & Drug Administration and National Institute of Health)...

Our research has shown that when we eat natural nutrients (at least 65% raw fruits and vegetables) there is an energy explosion within our body.

This gives the body the necessary tools it needs to rebuild strong cells that it takes to gain control of the body..."

—Dr. John H. Norris, Ph.D.,
Biochemist/ Microbiologist

One reading can change your life

On Saturday morning, May 23, 1998, I got up... and began to read "God's Way to Ultimate Health." That was a turning point in my life. One for which I will be eternally grateful. Over the next two days I literally devoured "God's Way..." I read and reread, underlined, turned down page corners, then read some more. There is so much information included inside the covers of this book, that there is no way to take it all in in just one reading. One reading can change your life though, as it did mine...

Today, approximately four and one half months later, I am 42 pounds lighter. I wear size 16 pants instead of 26 pants and 14-16 tops instead of 3x tops as I did when I began... I am able to walk without a cane, and without stumbling over myself... I am able to speak clearly and quickly without halting words... able to raise my arms straight above my head, which I had not been able to do for approximately ten years because of an injury to my rotator cuffs... able to think clearly and concisely again... able to get out of the bed in the morning without pain and stiffness due to Dr. diagnosed arthritis... able to stand and speak for hours at a time without having to sit and rest... absolutely NO pain in the arm in which I had surgery... able to read through strong eyes...

I've got my smile back.

AND I can sing and play the piano again!

All because of the loving mercy of God the Father, God the Son, and God the Holy Spirit, who introduced me to Rev. George H. Malkmus and revealed the wisdom and Godly counsel included in the Hallelujah Diet.

Judi Hurst

Aren't these testimonies wonderful? I can't tell you how eagerly I await each day's mail to learn of others who simply changed their diet and lifestyle and got well.

So if you are ready to learn more so that you can take charge of your health, please continue reading for the simple program that's reactivating immune systems all over the world.

The Hallelujah Diet and Lifestyle

Breakfast

One tablespoon of Barleygreen* powder either dry and let it dissolve in my mouth or in a couple of ounces of distilled water at room temperature. That is usually all I have until noon. If I do get hungry, then I may eat a piece of fresh juicy fruit later in the morning. Cooked food is an absolute no-no as my body is in a cleansing mode until about noon each day.

It is vitally important to me that the Barleygreen powder I use comes from American Image Marketing and that it contains kelp. There are other companies that have tried to imitate Barleygreen but they are not processed the same way. I have tried other products, but they do not give the same results. Nor do the Barleygreen caplets if swallowed. The caplets can be dissolved in the mouth like a lozenge, however. I enjoy them in this form, especially while traveling.

Lunch

One tablespoon of Barleygreen* powder, as at breakfast. Sometimes I stir my Barleygreen into eight ounces of freshly extracted carrot juice**, which I find especially delicious and extremely nutritious.

At least a half hour after the Barleygreen, I prefer an all-raw fruit lunch. A banana, apple, dates, etc. Organic is always best when available. (Sometimes I have a vegetable salad for lunch instead of the fruit.) It is important that this be an all raw meal.

Supper

One tablespoon of Barleygreen powder either dry or in a couple ounces of distilled water or in carrot juice. Carrot juice must be freshly extracted—never canned, bottled, frozen, or in powdered form.

Then, at least thirty minutes after the Barleygreen, I eat a large green vegetable salad of leaf lettuce (never head lettuce), broccoli, cauliflower, celery, carrots, etc. I enjoy adding half an avocado in most of my vegetable salads. This is usually followed by some cooked food (baked potato, baked sweet potato, brown rice, steamed vegetables, whole grain pasta, whole grain bread, and so on.)

Even a quick look at the recipes in "Recipes for Life... from God's Garden," will reveal there is nothing restrictive about supper on the Hallelujah Diet.

Later in the evening, I often have a glass of organic apple juice or a piece of juicy fruit.

(My diet consists of approximately 85 percent raw food and 15 percent cooked food.)

Exercise is also an essential part of my program. I do at least one hour of vigorous exercise daily. Additionally, I try to get some sunshine on as much of my body as possible every day.

To be sure I get the essential fatty acids needed by my body, I also have one tablespoon of Udo's Choice Perfected Oil Blend. I either have this on my evening salad or straight out of the bottle.

*The reason I supplement my diet with Barleygreen is that our food today is being grown for the most part on very deficient soils that often lack all the nutrients my body needs for building new, strong, healthy, vital, vibrant cells. Barleygreen contains the widest spectrum of nutrients available today from a single source that I am aware of. It is also loaded with enzymes. I consider it the single most important food I put in my body each day and always consume at least three tablespoons of it a day. Another AIM product I find very beneficial is Herbal Fiberblend, for added fiber, preventative maintenance of the colon, and insurance against parasitic infestations.

**The second most important thing I put into my body each day is freshly extracted carrot juice made from large California juicing carrots in a Green Power juicer. I try to drink at least 16 to 24 ounces each day. When I had my colon cancer more than 20 years ago, I consumed 32 to 64 ounces of carrot juice each day. If I had a serious physical problem today, I would consume up to eight 8-ounce glasses of carrot juice each day in addition to my three to four tablespoons of Barleygreen.

The reason Barleygreen and carrot juice is so important to me is:
1. Cooked food has practically no nutritional value.
2. A large percentage of the nutrients in raw food are lost in the digestion process, depending on the health of the digestive system.
3. When vegetable juices or Barleygreen is consumed, a high percentage of the nutrients reach cell level because the pulp has been removed and thus no digestion is necessary. Raw vegetable juices are the fastest way to nourish the cells and rebuild the immune system and essential body organs.

If you're like most people and, when you try the diet as taught above for even three weeks, you'll be amazed at how much better you feel. And that doesn't even mention the pounds you'll lose and the energy you'll gain.

Questions and Answers

Although our program is quite simple, we get a lot of questions. In this next section I want to share some common questions, along with brief answers.

I want to learn more. Do you have other articles I can read?

To better inform yourself about our program, you can subscribe to our free health magazine, *Back to the Garden,* by checking the subscription box and then returning the order form at the end of this book. Or you can read our books or listen to audio or watch video tapes or check out our wealth of free, informative articles online at http://www.hacres.com

My child has ADD. Will your diet help?

We have a number of reports from parents whose children had ADD and ADHD and were on Ritalin. After being on our program for various lengths of time, the children are now off medication, feeling fine, and having no more behavioral problems.

You see, we teach that when the body is fed and treated properly, in most cases it will adjust all systems to normal levels and heal what needs to be healed, no matter what the problem might be.

Why don't you eat breakfast?

We teach no breakfast so the body can continue to cleanse and detoxify until about noon each day. Skipping breakfast is also an excellent way to lose extra pounds rather painlessly.

Additionally, most people find they are much sharper mentally in the mornings if they're not using body energy to digest bacon and eggs, juice and toast, cereal and milk, or coffee and bagels.

For most people, a tablespoon of Barleygreen or a glass of carrot juice makes an excellent substitute for the SAD breakfast. This way you get pure nutrition that the body assimilates almost immediately with minimal energy expenditure.

Will the Hallelujah Diet cure my cancer, diabetes, MS, migraine headaches, and so on?

We have reports of improvement or healing of an incredible array of human ailments when people get on the Hallelujah Diet. Please see the testimonies in this book, in *Back to the Garden,* and on www.hacres.com for just a sampling of the reports we receive on a daily basis.

We teach that it doesn't matter what you've been diagnosed as having. The point is that God's self-healing immune system will probably solve your problem once you start eating and living according to His natural laws.

Sadly, we have to say "probably" because sometimes chemotherapy, radiation, surgery, and/or other powerful drugs have destroyed the immune system to the point where it is sometimes difficult to respond.

I take several shots a day of insulin. Can a diabetic like me get on the Hallelujah Diet?

Insulin-dependent diabetics need to consider transitioning carefully to the Hallelujah Diet. Individuals who have successfully made this transition report that they checked their blood sugar levels many times during the day and adjusted both their insulin and food intakes accordingly.

Some insulin-dependent diabetics had problems with carrot juice and had to either not use it or else use it diluted with distilled water or celery juice.

We encourage insulin-dependent diabetics to work closely with a nutritionally-aware physician if they aren't very confident of their own abilities to adjust their food and insulin needs according to their blood sugar readings.

We also encourage diabetics to limit their fruit intake. Some do best by not having any sweet fruits at all, especially when first transitioning.

Can I call Hallelujah Acres and receive a diagnosis and individualized health plan?

I'm sorry, but we cannot and do not diagnose or prescribe for anyone. Everyone is different and may react differently to our diet and lifestyle program, so all we can do is provide information about our program, point people to the testimonies, and then let them make informed decisions about how they want to best apply this knowledge.

To learn everything you need to know about our program, you can either learn for free from our website or else support our ministry by purchasing some of the books or tapes at the back of this publication.

Let me add that we see the best results in most people with health challenges when these people work our program 100% with no meat, no dairy, no white flour, no sugar, and no salt. These individuals also commit to getting some daily exercise, as well as Barleygreen and carrot juice.

It goes without saying that we encourage folks with serious health challenges to work closely with a nutritionally-aware physician.

I have a friend who needs your program. What can I do?

We'll gladly send information. Please contact the health minister who gave you this booklet or else send your friend's mailing address to us at: Hallelujah Acres, PO Box 2388, Shelby, NC 28151 or send an e-mail with the address to garden@hacres.com.

My doctor says I won't get enough calcium or protein on your diet. What do you say?

We say "nonsense" and urge you to have your doctor examine some of the results we're getting every day. For details on protein and calcium, see *God's Way to Ultimate Health* and/or *Recipes for Life... from God's Garden.* We also have articles on both subjects available for free on our website. Recent scientific findings reveal that all calcium and protein requirements can be adequately met on a pure vegetarian diet.

Our Health Ministry Program

At this point I'd like to mention some of our other excellent resources to help support your effort to improve your health and well-being.

When I started preaching the good news about the Hallelujah Diet, I knew I wouldn't be able to get this message to the entire world without help.

So in 1994 I started training Back to the Garden Health Ministers. As of November 1998, more than 1,500 men and women have come to Hallelujah Acres to learn about our program, and we currently have Health Ministers in all 50 states in the United States plus three provinces in Canada, as well as six foreign countries.

It is interesting to see how many are coming to our training from professional fields—seventeen medical doctors; four dentists; three optometrists; 43 chiropractors; and 104 registered nurses thus far. This large number of Christian health professionals coming to us for training is more understandable when you realize that 75 percent of the medical schools in America do not require a single course in nutrition for a medical degree.

We also have more than 300 pastors, evangelists, missionaries, and Sunday School teachers who have become Health Ministers, as well as housewives, construction workers, business leaders, and retired people. All of them want to help share the good news that "You don't have to be sick."

If you live in a large city, the chances are good that we have several health ministers there to help you.

To find a health minister near you, check the constantly-updated listing on our website or call Hallelujah Acres at 1-704-481-1700.

Here are some letters from health ministers who share why they decided to come to Hallelujah Acres for training:

I am a Christian and often wondered about people praying for healing from a 'lifestyle' disease while continuing the lifestyle that caused their problem. My first issue of Back to the Garden newsletter put it all together. God has given our bodies the ability to heal, but we must be good stewards of our bodies. This ministry is complete—spiritually and physically.

—Nancy Rigsby, Health Minister

I want to be a Health Minister in order to help people learn to treat the root problem and not the symptoms... I want to teach people how to eliminate sickness."

—Mary Glick, Health Minister

I want to be of service to mankind. I believe people need to be educated about the correlation of their health and what they eat. People need to be encouraged to learn about nutrition and its impact on their state of wellness. Since starting a living foods diet in May of 1993, my blood pressure is normal, legs no longer ache, I have lost 50 pounds, and have lots of energy.

Hiawatha Cromer, Health Minister

I feel that my career and life's experience so closely parallel that of George Malkmus that it has got to be God that arranged for me to hear about him. I want to spend the rest of my life helping people. I was personally healed of breast cancer on this program

Walter Clough, Health Minister

I have never been so excited or passionate about anything as much as your Hallelujah Acres ministry has moved me. I thank God every day, he led me to you. I have always been afraid of conventional medicine and I have seen deadly outcomes as a nurse. My husband is a medical physician and we both hope your message and understanding of God's principles will help us live a life of Godly character and minister and heal those whose lives we touch.

Carly M. Willeford, BSN, Health Minister

I worked as a pharmacist for six years and then opened my own pharmacy in 1979. The Lord blessed me and it grew into a $2 million a year business. I got disgusted seeing people destroyed with the drugs, so I sold the business and went into nutritional counseling.

Larry Rawdon, D.Ph., Health Minister

Here are a few letters from Health Ministers sharing the physical improvements they personally experienced after going on the Hallelujah Diet:

I had been on thyroid medication for six years and was told I would be on it for the rest of my life. But after 33 days on the Hallelujah Diet/Lifestyle... my doctor took me off the medication. I should also say I stopped all allergy shots and inhaler use and lost 25 lbs. And the reason we started this in March of 1996 was because of four surgeries (over a three-year period) to remove melanoma from my husband that kept recurring every eight months. We are thankful beyond words to say that he has remained cancer free for 21 months, as of January 1, 1998. We are now Health Ministers and Praise God for this program.

Lori Irby, Health Minister

In October of 1989 I was diagnosed with throat cancer. Two unsuccessful surgeries and 37 radiation treatments followed. The radiation treatments evidently lowered my immune system. Drainage from the sinus created severe laryngitis and I was unable to preach. I found myself with colds all the time and at the change of the season it seemed like a worse case of the flu. I was taking a prescription medication for sinus, a prescription medication for prostatitis, and 1600 milligrams of pain medication each day. I was also receiving cortisone injections in my shoulder for bursitis and arthritis.

In May of 1994, I began the Hallelujah Diet. Since then, I have taken no medication of any kind, not even an aspirin. My prescriptions were running $200 each month prior to this. All symptoms of all illnesses have disappeared, and I am healthier and feel better than I have in many years. I have no known health problems at 67 years of age: no cancer, no sinus problems, no prostatitis problems, no *laryngitis, no headaches, no bursitis, etc. Simply put, I am well! I now weigh 172 lbs at 6'1" height. A 54-lb loss from my high weight.*

All I did was follow George's advice and changed my diet. I recommend it to anyone. Try it... all you have to lose is your sickness.

Dr. J.C. House, Evangelist, Health Minister

I served 21 years in the U.S. Army all over the world... During that time I went from private to major. I was ill and your program brought me back to excellent health. I lost 15 pounds... The pain I had in my joints is gone. In my opinion, your program is the solution to our health problems in the United States. I enjoy helping people help themselves with the knowledge found in your program. It is a winner.

Charles S. Miller, Health Minister

On March 13, 1995, I had a second emergency surgery. My hemoglobin was down to 6.5 Another section of my small intestine was removed. This time the doctors called my problem 'Arterial Venous Malformation' or a malformation of the arteries and veins. For 25 days I laid in the hospital bed. My dear wife, Dian, slept 24 nights in a cot in my room, not knowing whether I would live or die. Altogether, over $100,000 in doctor and hospital bills were incurred.

During Tulsa's First Annual Prophecy Conference, Dr. Nathan Meyer, one of the speakers, came to visit me (at home) and prayed for me. He told what had happened to him on a diet called 'The Hallelujah Diet.' I had just had surgery, and I did nothing. I believed the surgery had cared for my problem. ONE MONTH LATER I STARTED BLEEDING AGAIN. Finally I went on the Hallelujah Diet on May 10, 1995. My internal bleeding started to slacken, but continued for about four months. Then it stopped and I have had no bleeding for almost three years. My most recent hemoglobin reading was 13.6"

—Dr. Charles Pack, Evangelist, Health Minister

[As of November, 1998, Dr. Pack is still not bleeding and in great health at age 80.]

Dear Rev. Malkmus:

We were told there was no cancer in the last C.A.T. scan. There was no cancer in the blood. These reports were given by our doctor to three other doctors for confirmation. We were told by the doctor that he had never seen cancer cured in three months in his practice. Frank did not have any medications, radiation, or chemotherapy. All of the reports are fully documented. We were wonderfully encouraged and told to keep doing what we were doing.

—Jan Owens, Health Minister

I am the Jail Minister who recently gave testimony at your seminar about the **cancer** *under my tongue and how I rejected the massive tongue clipping and radical neck dissections recommended three different times by three different physicians.*

When I fasted and prayed five days in January, God took me to Genesis 1:29. But I did not know what to do about it until a friend sent me to your seminar in February.

Since then, the Hallelujah Diet has stopped my cancer growth and I am off my cholesterol medicine for the first time in 15 years. I am also no longer **hypoglycemic** and no longer need PeptoBismol or Preparation H. Glory to God!

They gave me 6 to 8 months to live, and I have never felt better or had better energy in my whole life. I am no longer conformed to the world's way of eating...

My son, after seeing the improvement in my health, asked if I felt this diet could help him get off his **Ritalin**. He said he was embarrassed each day at school when he had to stand in line with other students to receive his Ritalin during Ritalin breaks.

Well, he went on the Hallelujah Diet and no longer has any need for Ritalin. Hallelujah!

—Rev. Alfred Lewis, Health Minister

And finally, here are some typical results seen by our Health Ministers in the lives of others as they share the Hallelujah Diet and program in their churches and communities:

One lady was in her early 50's. She suffered from lupus, diabetes, fibromyalgia, arthritis, and was very obese. She is a nurse. After four months on your program she had lost 50 lbs. She was off insulin and off the 14 other medications, including pain medication, and was able to do about 30 minutes of aerobic exercise daily. Previously she had not even been able to tie her own shoes.

Tom and Laurie Ousley, Health Ministers

Lupus gone; diabetes gone; colon tumors disappeared; female troubles improved; MS improved; mercury poisoning and psoriasis cleared up... not enough hours in the day to meet the demand.

Rev. Brian W. Cutts, Health Minister

Many senior citizens in church are off their medications, lost weight, and are more active than they have been in years. Chronic migraines completely gone in several; one lady's arthritis is gone and her fingers are returning to normal.

Nancy Rigsby, Health Minister

Diabetics getting sugar under control; lots of weight loss; more energy, psoriasis clearing up; people are infused with hope which has healing in it.

Bev Cook, Health Minister

Seventy-year old off shots after 10 years of insulin dependence; liver disease in remission.

Nancy Fitzmorris, Health Minister

Diabetes gone; arthritis reversed; lumps gone; prostate cancer gone; no more migraines.

Bob and Karen King, Health Ministers

Whole family plus in-laws on program. Father, overweight all his life, has dropped 60 lbs. Both children and father suffered with severe sinus and allergy problems and have been helped.

Dr. Rowen Pfeifer, Health Minister

Allergies relieved; diabetes lessened; high blood pressure gone; cancer patient helped; arthritis relief and general feelings of well being.

Janet and Fred Huhn, Health Ministers

Currently helping a recovered diabetic... Doctors wanted to amputate his legs, but he went on the Hallelujah diet and lost 180 lbs... still has both legs and Dr. will take him off medication on next visit.

Helmut and Ingred Joks, Health Ministers

Weight loss, prostate cancer, and arthritis healed. Children who get off dairy... have no more ear infections, sinus infections, no more antibiotics, no more colds, flus, no more seasonal allergies.

Carol Cover, Health Minister

MS patient doing very well. Lymphatic cancer patient completely back to normal, young mother with two small children on program to remain healthy. Many lowered blood pressure and blood sugar, etc.

Osa Anderson, Health Minister

A heart attack patient now walks three to five miles per day after beginning the Hallelujah Diet and is the picture of health at the age of 74. Most people are more energetic and happy about the change in their attitude as well as physical health.

Dr. Wojciech Wojcik, Health Minister

Help for diabetes, high blood pressure, diverticulosis, weight, pain, energy, gum disease.

Rev. Brice Casey, Health Minister

In the coming years we envision tens of thousands of Christians creating their own Health Ministries all around the world. Not only will many individuals want to become involved, but every pastor and church should become a part, for the sake of the health of their own membership as well as to use this information in an outreach ministry in their community. Pastors and evangelists across America as well as missionaries around the world are already incorporating the health message into their ministries, much to the benefit of their congregations. Some pastors have told us that large percentages of their congregations are on the Hallelujah Diet and that they hardly ever have prayer requests for sickness anymore.

After you've tried our program and have experienced its results, you might want to become a health minister in your church or community. For details about our training program, send an e-mail to ministry@hacres.com or call or write and request our Health Ministry information packet.

You mean it's that simple?

Many people find it hard to believe that the human body can heal itself so quickly and so thoroughly and so simply. In fact, we hear all the time from people who don't try it straight off because it sounds too easy to them.

Well, my friend, the proof is in the pudding.

Why not try our program for three short weeks to see if it won't work the wonders for you that it's working for tens of thousands of others?

Although the Hallelujah Diet and Lifestyle stands alone as a great "do it your-self" program, remember we also have a support system in place which includes over 1,500 trained health ministers across the U.S. and Canada and in six foreign countries, as well as a large website on the Internet where you can get free details 24 hours a day.

In closing, my friend, Hallelujah Acres exists as a ministry to spread to the world the message "You don't have to be sick."

Please try our program in your life and experience its benefits.

And after you've done so, we urge you to help us share with suffering human-ity the good news—*You don't have to be sick.*

God bless you.

Sincerely for a Healthy World,

Rev. George H. Malkmus

P.S. Although I've explained in these pages everything you need to know to reactivate your immune system and to start building yourself a better body, many people will want additional details before beginning. We have some great resources for you, and you'll find them starting on page 46.

Are you a Christian?

Although this book was written primarily for Christians, it is possible, dear reader, that you are not a true, Bible Christian. If not, please consider that you can apply all the principles of this book and live a long, healthy life but spend eternity separated from God and heaven. If this is your case, God's good news is that the Lord Jesus Christ shed His sinless blood as the full, finished payment for sin, was buried and rose again for our justification. By placing our faith and trust in Him and His blood alone, we are saved, born from above, become a new creature in Christ and headed for an eternity in heaven! Will you place your faith in Christ now? (If you will, please write me, and I will send you more Biblical information to help you in your walk with Christ.)

Hallelujah Acres Resource Guide

Back to the Garden is our 28 page, semi-annual, health magazine. It is just loaded with helpful information, additional testimonies, recipes and what is happening at Hallelujah Acres. Current circulation is approximately 200,000 and is sent out FREE of charge to all who request it.

Hallelujah Health Tip (currently over 10,000 subscribers) is our free e-mail newsletter that goes out over the Internet every week. With tips about how to do our program, as well as recipes and testimonials, this publication is enjoyed by health seekers all over the world. Send an e-mail to subscribe@hacres.com to get on the list.

Why Christians Get Sick by Rev. George Malkmus is very helpful in introducing Christians to a natural diet and lifestyle. Letters are received daily from all over the world from people helped by this book, which is now in its 20th printing. *Why Christians Get Sick* is written on a solid Biblical foundation with over 150 Bible verses. This was Rev. Malkmus' first book. (Paperback, $8.95)

God's Way to Ultimate Health by Rev. George Malkmus with Michael Dye has everything you need to know about how to return to God's original plan for nourishing the human body. Read what the Bible says about diet and how this Biblical wisdom is supported by modern science and hundreds of real life testimonials. Also an entire section of recipes and tips by Rhonda Malkmus on how to set up your own natural foods kitchen. *God's Way to Ultimate Health* contains 282 pages of vital information that has changed the way thousands of people think about what they put into their bodies. Many people say this book has saved their lives. (Perfect bound paperback, $18.95)

Recipes for Life... from God's Garden by Rhonda Malkmus is the perfect companion piece to *God's Way to Ultimate Health* because it begins where the theory and rationale for the diet leaves off. With more than 400 nutritious and delicious recipes, this huge 8 1/2 by 11-inch spiralbound book is already treasured in tens of thousands of kitchens. Healthy food tastes wonderful, and this book proves it. Has important chapters on how to feed children and young adults, along with menus and even a section on feeding babies. Detailed index lists recipes not only by chapter but also alphabetically. (Spiral bound, $24.95)

Twenty-One Days to Health the Hallelujah Diet Way — Chet Day takes you by the hand in this 104-page book and shows you exactly what you need to do on a daily basis for twenty-one days to move from the Standard American Diet to the energy-filled, healthy Hallelujah Diet and lifestyle. Just about everyone who goes on this program for three weeks makes a commitment to stay on it because they feel so good. A fabulous buy. Priced to get copies for friends and family. ($4.95)

How to Eliminate Sickness Video —This professionally-produced video was shot on-site in Tulsa, Oklahoma, at the Tulsa Bible Prophecy Conference. The 2 1/2 hour seminar contains much updated information not available in our earlier videotapes, including Bible Scripture and current research in traditional medicine as well as alternative health. This is an up-to-date version of the seminar Rev. Malkmus has delivered across the United States and Canada. It covers the basics of why we get sick and how to nourish our bodies to restore our health. It will change your thinking forever as to what is nutrition and what is not. You must see this remarkable video. ($24.95)

How to Eliminate Sickness Audio —This two-cassette audio was take from the soundtrack of the above "How to Eliminate Sickness" Video. This is a dynamic presentation of the health message from a Biblical perspective. This recording has much new information not available in previous recordings. (Two tapes in jacket, $12.95)

Testimonial Video—Filmed at the Tulsa Bible Prophecy Conference, this moving video features 5-minute testimonies of 13 men and women who healed themselves of a remarkable variety of illnesses by going on the Hallelujah Diet. This video contains testimonies by a medical doctor, nurses, preachers, and folks from many walks of life. If you know someone who resists the "You don't have to be sick" message, this tape of testimonials will open their hearts to the truth of the power of the Hallelujah Diet. ($14.95)

Children and the Hallelujah Diet—In April of 1998, Dr. Joel Robbins shared with health ministers what he'd learned about health and children. In this tape of his address on the subject, you'll learn why you're letting your family down if you don't get your kids on a healthy diet. Dr. Robbins also provides helpful suggestions on how to get your children on a living diet as well as how to keep them there. ($9.95)

The China Project—A scientific study of the most comprehensive survey ever conducted on the relationship between diet and disease. Highly recommended. (32 pages, $3.50)

Y2K the Hallelujah Acres Way—Rev. George Malkmus reveals how you can remain healthy and happy on the Hallelujah Diet during potential Y2K disruptions. Individuals, churches, and community groups will find this booklet very helpful. (32 pages, $2.95)

Quantity Discounts — A Christian Health Primer

Number of Copies	Price		Number of Copies	Price
1–3 books	$3.95 each		4–10 books	$3.16 each
11–49 books	$2.77 each		50–499	$2.37 each

Customer Order Form

Shipping Charges

$5 for all orders under $50. Add 10% for orders over $50. Call for foreign rates outside of the Continental U.S. North Carolina residents, please add 6% sales tax to entire order.

Return Policy

No returns accepted without an RMA number. Call 1-704-481-1700 from 8-5 Monday through Friday for details.

Name: _____

Address: _____

City: _____ State: _____ Zip: _____

Phone: (_____) _____

Please provide a physical address–not a P.O. Box–for UPS delivery.

☐ Please check if you are not on our mailing list, and would like a free subscription to *Back to the Garden*.

Qty.	Item #	Item Name	Price Each	Total

☐ Check ☐ Money Order ☐ Visa ☐ MC   Sub–total

☐ Discover ☐ American Express   6% Sales Tax (NC residents only)

Card Number: _____   Shipping

Signature: _____   **TOTAL**

Card Exp. Date _____

How to Reach Us

U.S.

Credit Card Orders Call: (704) 481-1700
Mail Orders to: Hallelujah Acres
P.O. Box 2388
Shelby, NC 28151
Fax: (704) 481-0345 • **Website:** www.hacres.com

Canada

Credit Card Orders Call: (519) 935-9999
Mail Orders to: Hallelujah Acres Canada
P.O. Box 7, RR 2
Shallow Lake ONT N0H 2K0
Fax: (519) 935-3044 • **Website:** www.hacres.com